LEARN

TO

LEAD

BY SERVING

Seven lessons that will transform
your leadership and help you become
the leader you aim to be!

DUSTIN DALE

I want to foremost give credit and glory to God. My life has been shaped and transformed by the lessons and teaching He has provided to me. I wouldn't have been able to write this book without His wisdom and direction.

I also want to thank every team and team member I had the privilege of leading over the past ten years. All of you were the inspiration behind this book. Without you, my success wouldn't mean a thing.

TABLE OF CONTENTS

MY STORY

I feel it's important for every leader to be transparent and to share something from their life that changed them or shaped why they chose to become a leader. I have always encouraged the leaders I've trained over the years to never be afraid to share why they are passionate about being a leader. The story you're about to read is what started my whole mindset of thinking differently. At the time, I was unaware it would lead me to writing this book later in life.

When I was nine, I found myself lying in a hospital bed, with doctors making rounds every half hour to ensure I was still alive. The only thing I knew at the time was I was told to move as little as possible and if my nose started to bleed, I had to call the nursing team immediately. The fear that haunted the medical staff was that if I started to bleed, there may not be a hope of stopping it. How at age nine are you supposed to stay completely still? Your whole purpose as a child is to enjoy playing and to make fond memories that you reflect on later in your life. It's not to face the fact that your life may not allow you to look back, as you may be at your ultimate point.

The only things I could piece together as memories were the smells all around me. To this day, I can still smell the bland food that was on my tray because of the special diet I needed to be on. This food was much easier to throw up when the medicine hit my system, and it didn't burn as bad when it came up. It was also a source of nutrients, or so the doctor said. All I knew was I didn't really understand what was going on or why I was there.

The first hospital team who treated me had no clue what was wrong with me, so they decided to perform two bone marrow tests to start the process of elimination. However, the answer they landed on would prove incorrect later down the road. I remember the doctor walking into my room with a file in his hand. He wasn't a very emotional man and had a very dry speaking voice. His exact words were, "Well, there's no point in beating around the bush. Your son seems to have leukemia, and it's aggressive."

When you're nine, you have no idea that word even exists until you hear it come from a doctor's mouth, and even then, you still have no reference for what it means. You especially don't understand it means possible death if not treated. You don't know why your mother and father look like they have seen a ghost. The worst part about being sick when you're so young is that no one tries to explain to you what's wrong; they just tell you something is wrong. I couldn't grasp what was happening inside my body, at least not at first.

They started me on chemotherapy right away, which was the typical course for the standard treatment of leukemia. Again, I had no clue what that word *chemotherapy* meant or how violent it was on a nine-year-old body. The problem was the medical team had no idea that what they were fighting wasn't what was expected. It wasn't their fault, as the problem I had wasn't common and was extremely rare in the number of cases that were diagnosed. They were following the protocol to the best of their knowledge, and I'm grateful for their efforts to keep me alive.

The chemotherapy began to take its toll, and my journey started that first day. The smell of the IV fluid flush is one I still can recall to this day. What I didn't know at the time was this would prepare me for a road of many more needles and IVs I would have to face. As the treatments started to run their course in my body, so did the progression of problems that come with chemo.

I can recall the stomach acid burning so badly as it came up in the middle of the night because I was too weak to eat anything and every bit of food I did eat always came up hours later anyway. My weight dropped quickly, and I soon found myself literally skin and bones. But the understanding of what was happening started to form in my mind. I started to change—I began seeing and thinking differently. When you are nine and are going through this scary situation, your mind finds every feasible way to block the pain and create a story for you to feel better about.

When I turned twelve, the greatest miracle happened. We figured out what was wrong with my body after a visit to Duke Raleigh Hospital in Raleigh, North Carolina. After a couple of blood tests and cross-checking all the treatments I had undergone, they were able to determine I was born with an autoimmune disease called ITP or idiopathic thrombocytopenic purpura. This disease disguises itself as cancer in children, based on the result of a blood test. Fortunately, testing has greatly evolved since my childhood.

With ITP, the body attacks the platelets that are produced by the spleen. The reason they are attacked is because when the body makes those platelets, they are "marked" or "highlighted" as a virus or some form of infection. If your body destroys too many platelets, you are at an extreme risk of bleeding, especially internal bleeding. When you get a cut or a scrape or even a nosebleed, the process of clotting that happens is because your platelets get together and begin to repair the injury. The healing takes place when they form a wall. When you have too few platelets to form a wall, you continue to bleed, including spontaneous internal bleeding.

The treatment Duke was able to steer me toward was a specialized one that would help slow down the process of my immune system killing the platelets. After three rounds of infusions with IVIG (intravenous immunoglobulin), my body began to reset itself. The average level for a human is between 150,000–400,000. At the time I was admitted to the hospital, my platelets were hovering at less than 2,000.

As I reported for weekly blood tests to monitor the situation, the process of my healing began. This was when I started to understand that my journey would be defined by how I chose to live my life from this point on. I knew I was saved and was left on this earth to give back, just like all the doctors and nurses who ensured a nine-year-old boy didn't die. I fully understood this was the starting point of what I would later develop as my leadership.

Those years served a greater purpose in my life, and you can't always connect the dots when you're trying to look ahead. You can only connect them after you have gained your wisdom, your experiences, and the maturity to see clearly in the rearview mirror. Those years would light a fire in me to become focused on changing lives and caring for others. I had my difficulties like everyone, but I never regret going through what I did at an early age. I'm extremely thankful for those lessons I learned.

INTRODUCTION

I t is important to know why I focus so much on my leadership, and the only way I can tell you is by being transparent about my journey. We all have been through that pivotal point in our lives where we found ourselves at the crossroads of our futures. Sometimes individuals navigate through life on a smooth and seamless path to success, but others find it through failing and self-discovery.

Some of us were presented with a different path and sometimes not by our choosing. In order for you to gain the knowledge from these lessons, I want to share that the previous ten years of my career have been a daily focus on growing my development surrounding my leadership. The interesting part of leadership is that it never stops and it's a continuous path you walk your entire life. To this day, I still find myself on the path of development and continued growth as a leader in my daily reflections based on these seven servant leadership lessons.

The seven lessons in this book were the most vital to my success, and I used them to lead over one thousand employees during my ten-year career and to guide over one hundred leadership teams that reported directly to me. I wish I could tell you that every lesson in this book was the magic formula to my success, but I can't. The foundation for these lessons was how they helped shape my mind and how I saw myself. They were the mirror that allowed me to see myself as the leader I was.

In my initial stages of becoming a leader, I didn't know what I didn't know, and it was a good thing I started at the bottom of the chain of command. Starting at the bottom afforded me the time to focus on learning what I needed to. My first job that led into my career wasn't a leadership role; in fact, it was about the lowest position you could have in the organization. I started my career as a seasonal employee, and I don't mean the term *low* as in authority. Being a seasonal hire meant you were temporary if you didn't make the cut or if you were just looking to make some quick cash for a short season. Though like in many success stories we've heard, I chose the path of resilience and perseverance. I had my fair share of learning moments, but the bumpy path was the greatest experience that I now look back on and understand how it led to my becoming a leader. It led to a life of service.

Think about the greatest winning teams and success stories we all have heard. A common relationship every story share is the legend of the great coach who led to their victories. The strongest team in terms of skill can be the worst winning team if there is no one to guide them. That coach knows exactly how to train their team—they focus on the strengths and know how to develop the weaknesses. Therefore, I want to offer you training and knowledge in developing strong leadership. I want you to become the success story of your team.

Leadership is the ability to connect with people in a way that influences and guides them. I want this book to serve as an interactive guide that inspires you and builds you up so you're able to apply it all in a way that fits you. Beyond that, you should feel enthusiastic about your progression from a good leader to a great one.

Leadership is about being able to creatively direct people, organizations, and communities toward success. It's wise for you to be authentic in your approach and to discover multiple methods that will work for you. Often, circumstance decides which style you'll need and how you'll apply it. Sometimes using a more direct approach is required. However, if you push too hard, you could lose the trust of your team, which is the most valuable key to success. The greatest coaches all shared a bonded trust between themselves and the members of their team.

I wanted to share this guide with you because I was blessed to work under great leaders and increase my knowledge during my personal journey. It took a lot of hardships, highs, and lows for me to be able to accept that I'll never have every answer, but it's good to be humble and keep a willingness to learn. Early in my career when I took a role in leading others, I found myself making decisions on my own without any input. I failed to seek guidance from those who could have helped me, including my leaders. This created a trust issue when it came time for me to lead them. I thought I was doing the right thing because I believed the leader always had to speak, to give direction, and to take all the credit. I was naïve in my understanding of being a true servant leader. I was playing the victim to pressure from the higher levels to achieve success quickly, so I used that as an excuse to cover my bad decision-making. I will tell you now, ten years later, to avoid this at all costs.

Honestly, I felt like I was doing a great job for the company until it was proved otherwise. What I didn't pay attention to was how I was making every decision without any long-term thought. I was damaging the brand by telling people where to go and what to do without stopping and analyzing the correct information needed to make informed decisions. Going through these lows allowed me to slow down, and I began studying what it meant to be a foundational leader. Being able to stop and reflect on what was happening gave me a desire to learn more about being an effective leader and prompted me to share the knowledge I was gaining through my own failures. Great leaders like us can apply what we're learning in order to do our best. There are so many professionals who are enthusiastic about what they do and want to be the best they can be. I want to guide you along the way.

I won't call it my secret recipe, but I will tell you that the seven lessons I expand on in this guide will set a solid foundation for you to use to build your house of leadership and knowledge. I feel these are the keys to developing and progressing through our lives not just from a leadership standpoint but from a personal one as well. It took me the longest time to understand that leadership wasn't a finish line but a marathon that never ended. It was learning that I needed to be aware of my character and where I cast my shadow.

The beauty of this guide is what you make of it. This book could be the inspiration you need in your life to keep the ball rolling. I have laid out exercises and sections to journal throughout the book. Some have multiple sections to complete, while others will spark the contemplation to do so. What you take from this book and apply to your life and career will reward you in the end.

Lastly, I want to thank you for purchasing this book and believing in me. This guide was inspired by all the amazing leaders I worked with and the teams I was blessed to manage. They motivated me during some of the most difficult moments in my career. Those relationships kept me moving forward when I felt I was going in reverse. I want to pass on the beauty of knowledge and resourcefulness that you can use to improve your leadership and start building those relationships. Think of someone who could benefit from this guide, and don't hesitate to share it with them too.

LESSON ONE
FOCUS ON YOU

As this lesson title states, we will be starting from the source of all leadership—you! Reflection is vital to our individual and business successes. There is a significant benefit to understanding yourself before you lead your teams or organization. We must do the inner work first because great leaders know when it's necessary to step up and hold themselves accountable on a higher level.

I know now that before I could have ever led anyone in my career or life, I needed to fully understand how my mind worked and how underdeveloped my emotional intelligence was. This was one of the hardest areas for me to develop, and it continues to be a focused practice to this day. The reason why this lesson is ongoing is because I didn't realize that leadership wasn't a "one size fits all" approach. I figured that if I led one person in a way that was somewhat successful, then I could lead everyone else in the same direction. When I first started my journey toward leadership, I didn't really grasp the importance of learning how my mind worked or how I came to make my decisions.

There were practices and exercises I focused on that helped me comprehend the knowledge of what it took to develop my mind, so I was equipped to lead others. The first exercise I want to lead you through is going to give you a foundation to build your skillset for how you think and make your decisions

Imagine you're in a room that's quickly filling up with water and that there are others with you. In this situation, you're the only one who can save these people by helping them escape. Now imagine that they can't swim but you must ensure they make it safely out of the room. The oxygen is dwindling, and you have one minute left to decide how you will help everyone get out.

What would your approach be to get everyone to safety in a short amount of time? Panic is high, and you're running out of time, so asking people for their input won't be very helpful. Water is crashing in like waves, and nobody can hear you. Maybe you rely on one or two strong listeners to help you demonstrate how to swim. Again, you're the leader, and they are counting on you to lead them out safely.

Take a couple of minutes to write down your plan. What approach would you take? Immerse yourself in this situation, force your mind to think under pressure, and write.

Plan of Action

I'll never see your plan, but there is no better person to examine this than you. I wish I learned sooner to reflect on how my mind worked under pressure. I didn't realize how important it was for me to look back and connect the dots to understand what I aimed to achieve. Let's start with some logical observations.

Checking for a window, a door, or an opening in the room that would allow water to evacuate would be the logical thing to do first. That's why leaders with a direct approach would think to go for an exit first. However, for this exercise, that possibility is far too simple. The quickest answer doesn't always result in a larger reward and could potentially cost you more in the end. I found myself in this loop of quick decision-making without taking all information and factors into consideration.

In one example I can recall, there was a massive project due, and the timeline to achieve the desired result was extremely short. Again, I thought the leader had to be the one making all the decisions and giving all directions. I fell into the trap of getting too bogged down in every detail that I ended up missing the deadline. I should have stopped, and delegated tasks based on the strengths of my leaders. I failed to build trust with them because I needed to make decisions quickly.

Let us return to the drowning scenario. The water is rushing in, but we spot a window in the room and start to tread toward it. How are you going to open the window? Have you thought about what you'll do if you're unable to pull it up or slide it open? What could you use to break the window, and how far away is this object? People are counting on your next move to save their lives. I pray this never happens, but I believe you can learn something from this.

When you decide quickly without thinking forward and put yourself in what-if scenarios, you may jeopardize yourself or someone else. Making a conscious choice is hard to do in pressing situations. I understand the stress of needing to prove you're capable of leadership, but I always thought a majority of that forced me to make fast decisions. It wasn't until failing in those moments that I started to recognize the importance of considering all my options. These are the lessons that construct your ability to lead well.

The following question goes to the next point: do I have enough time to consider every option in this situation? In the earlier paragraph, it may seem like I'm telling you to take your time when making decisions, and sometimes you have to, but I want you to see what can happen when you're slow to decide.

As the room is filling up with water, you go to each person and ask them for their personal preference on how to open the object to let the water out. You ask these simple questions: Do you think you'll be ready if the water rushes out? Can you hold your breath long enough for the water to exit? Do you think you can make it through the area where the water is leaving? While you're taking time to get everyone's thoughts, you're losing sight of how the water is rising, and even though you're trying to ensure everyone has voiced their thoughts, you'll still lose someone because of the time you took. I also found myself learning from this situation, as I realized I was making decisions too fast.

I then made a change to put more time into my thoughts, which isn't always a terrible thing, but I still "lost" some members of my team. I was so scared of reverting to the old way that I did a 180 and found myself stuck in this new method of thinking. There were times when I lost sight of how important it was to put a timeline on the response, and some of my teams felt I almost didn't care because of how long it took to get to them. I was focused on circling back to everyone who gave me an opinion, and I forgot some of the individuals along the way, as there were too many. The funny thing is my intentions were the opposite, so let that be a takeaway for you. Learn to ask those who can provide solutions and are consistent with their feedback and ideas. This will keep you from making my mistake of trying to remember a lengthy list of names.

I felt so enthusiastic about making sure everyone had their opportunity to speak that I lost sight of not being able to speak to everyone at once. I failed to utilize some basic common forms of communication, such as group meetings or team huddles with key individuals. I was too afraid that if I gave too much attention to one person during a meeting, the others would feel less valued. You'll find yourself doing the same at some point during your time as a leader. I would like to stress that taking this time is okay, but always pay attention to your surroundings to ensure you're not taking too long.

At this point in the water scenario, you should be asking yourself what the best answer is. What I need you to remember is a guide to help you become comfortable with yourself and the leadership traits you own. We're aiming to have you become more familiar with yourself and how to guide your leadership in the best direction by getting to know you better.

In the table below, I want you to write down how you're feeling at this point based on the options we have talked about. Do you rush the water out, or do you take the time to seek everyone's opinion and explain the situation? Write down how you feel about the situation versus writing down your solution. Are you upset there isn't a clear path? Or are you confident your answer is the right choice?

Thoughts and Feelings

When you're writing your response, I want you to see how collected your thoughts are and how you're feeling about them. It's extremely hard to understand how we rationalize our actions sometimes if we don't write down the mechanics of our thoughts and see them through our eyes instead of our minds in order to understand our concepts. It took me a couple years to understand I had more success when I took the time to slow down and write out my ideas versus just keeping them in my mind.

Remember when I said we would talk about why the best person to see what you're writing is yourself? The point made above is for that reason. So often we are looking for approval from our boss or direct leader, our peers, and so on. Sometimes we feel embarrassed to write anything down because we fear judgment. Never let the fear of judgment keep you from asking a question or writing down notes. I was guilty of this early in my career because I felt my "presence" needed to be that of an expert.

This guided book is great in this regard because I want to help you feel comfortable that you can write down what you think your actions are without feeling like there's a teacher over your shoulder. As leaders, what we do in private will always be seen in public. You can't wake up and fake making good decisions.

The point of the exercise above and of writing down your thoughts is to have you see yourself by how you think. When you take a leadership position, you must change your mind and how you view the world and situations. This doesn't mean you need to do a total overhaul and become someone different, but if you don't adapt as you grow stronger and reach new levels, the old phrase will be true, "What got you here won't take you there."

I certainly understood that what got me my first leadership role wouldn't carry through when I was running the largest operation of my career years down the road. Now, what landed me my first leadership role was extremely challenging work. In fact, no one around me worked harder than I did to present a great-looking department with massive sales. What I failed to understand as I progressed was the higher I climbed, the more I needed to learn to delegate more and work less. I needed to focus more attention on teaching and training others to be leaders, not taskers. Once I learned this lesson, it helped me with running a business with over five hundred employees and thirty direct line leaders. There was no way I could've succeeded if I didn't focus on teaching and training. I had to adapt and understand that while the key basics were there, I needed to search for and learn ways of continued growth.

There are a couple of key principles I want to call out with our water-in-the-room scenario before we move on. The first principle is in the situation of handling others. I want you to feel the pressure of the decision on your shoulders and your mind running through many different answers. This "pressure cooker" feeling is a crazy emotion that can derail even the best leaders because their minds weren't conditioned to feel comfortable with handling pressure.

Again, it starts with your mind and the control of your emotions and reactions. There will be those in the room who begin to panic right away; they feel like the end is already the reality. If you panic along with them, the whole room won't make it, or a new leader will appear. Don't lose your confidence or control.

I want you to take a couple of minutes and write down a time when you had to decide or give guidance and you panicked too quickly. Did you find yourself falling into the pressure of diverting away from your original concept? Did someone become upset, and you followed their reaction with the same response? Don't feel embarrassed to write down the situation or feel like it was wrong to react the way you did. This is to help you see how you think. Be honest.

What was the situation?

The importance of this exercise is to understand that I don't want you to feel defeated about reliving a decision in the past. I strongly believe that you can't live in your past because it'll always keep you from your future. However, there is beauty in learning and reflecting to ensure that if you make a mistake, then you can course-correct it.

Imagine the first physical signs of panic: your heart starts to beat a little faster, and you breathe through your mouth instead of your nose. If you learn to catch these triggers early, then you stand a better chance of gaining control over your emotions. Your mind starts racing because it's looking for comfort; it doesn't like to feel weird or lost, so it focuses on something you feel okay with. When you start to feel these triggers in your daily leadership position, realize these are lessons in disguise, which is a beautiful thing.

The more you feel comfortable with controlling those thoughts and training your mind to feel at ease when things don't line up, the better and stronger your decisions will become. This is how you condition your mind to be prepared for uncertainty.

This exercise has been a huge help in my personal life when I needed to make complex decisions. As I wrote down how I would rationalize the decision, I really began to see how my mind was working because it was a live document sitting in front of me. That's why I strongly encourage the practice of writing out your decisions or jotting down bullet points that will help you decide. It'll keep your mind sharp!

Over time sharp knives become dull, hence the invention of the knife sharpener to bring a dull blade back to its full potential. I think the miracle drug, if invented, would be a pill to restore our minds so we could remember everything we need and all the wonderful memories of youth. Sadly, that pill will never exist, as we're meant to age and our minds age with us, but there are exercises we can do to stay mentally sharp.

The reason I'm touching on the point of staying mentally sharp is that our leadership abilities and actions are no different than our minds. Imagine you have the fastest racehorse in your pasture; however, you never ride it, you never focus on its diet, and there is no daily activity to keep it at its prime. That racehorse will no longer be the fastest after a while because it begins to accept what is now slowly becoming its unique environment. The horse will slowly process that the days of running, daily exercise, and a precision diet are no longer in place. Its new daily routine is passing the time in the stable with two to four meals a day. This is the starting point for the greatest horse of all time to become a "remember that horse" conversation.

Our minds are exactly like this, and we must understand how important it is to keep a focus on our mental status, especially with leadership. The key here is leadership is an ongoing knowledge tool. It's not something you learn once, and then you can never brush up on it again, just like a knife becomes dull because of use. The world is evolving, and so is leadership in our workplace environments, especially with the advancement of technology and how quickly individuals can access data. The fact-checking tools are in full force because now anyone with a smartphone, tablet, or computer can use it to reference just about anything.

Keeping your skills at the forefront of your focus will help you from becoming the "remember that leader" conversation. Your mind is the horse; when you're motivated and eager to go, you know exactly what to do. That is your current environment, but please pay attention to that key piece of information. Something you read or studied is honing your knowledge, and now you're applying that practice just like the daily drills for the racehorse. The diet for your mind is the continuing studies.

Imagine now that you stop reading about leadership; you find yourself reading only ten to fifteen minutes a week instead of one to three hours. The conditioning of your mind has started, and this is normal. The trick is to remember that there is always something new you can learn, read, or understand. When we begin to think we're mastering something, we slowly take time away from that subject. That's why we have professional athletes, actors, speakers, and so on. They are the individuals who constantly stay on top of their practice and training. You have the exact same control they do; there is no difference except in how quickly you realize you're slipping and motivate yourself back into studying what is needed.

Our last exercise of the chapter is a routine-building practice to sharpen your mind. I want to challenge you to create five key actions you think you need to take weekly or monthly to sharpen your mental skills around leadership. You could retake an old course and challenge yourself to look for a new lesson. You could aim to read one to two hours of published articles on leadership. The key here is this is meant for you to take time to focus on yourself and where you think you can improve. Take as much time as you need and write down those five actions. Once you have them written down, start with number one and complete them. Mark them off or write them in pencil so you can create five new actions next time.

Actions

Excellent job on writing those down! Now when you're mentally focused, you can discover how you think during a stressful decision-making time and how your mind works by seeing your thought process through difficulties. You now have shown five key actions you can take to keep your mind sharp about leadership.

It's important that before you move on to the next lesson of this book, you reflect on the exercises above and ensure you were 100 percent honest with the answers you wrote down. I really challenge you to put everything you have into this guide.

Finish this chapter by saying the following aloud three times: *I am awesome. I am sharp. I am confident!*

LESSON TWO
SERVE BELOW AND
WIN ABOVE

Welcome to the next step on your journey of guiding your leadership. I hope you took the time to really embrace and practice focusing on understanding yourself and your decision-making thought process during lesson one. I want to encourage you to revisit the lesson if you need to reference your thoughts or actions. In fact, I'd encourage you to take five minutes a day to review the questions and your responses, not just to remember those answers but to reflect upon them. You may find that you'll change your answers or even see a new way of looking at the situation as you evolve with this guide. One of the many beauties of leadership is seen when we gain more experience in our decision-making and thought process. Then we can look back and have a better understanding of another route that could have been taken—a more effective and successful approach.

Lesson two will bring a change in direction from lesson one, as we will move from focusing on you to focusing on your team or organization. The lesson title gives a quick but clear description as to what we'll focus on during this lesson: "Serve below and win above." I will lead you through the journey and focus on developing your understanding of how you can serve your team, with key principles about your leadership, communication, and enthusiasm. I want you to learn the importance of focusing on your teams based on servant leadership practices. I want us to fully embrace and immerse ourselves in these principles, not rush through them. Instead, take the time to reflect on them and learn. This will help you promote an interactive environment. It will also change your focus as you approach new situations and see more than one route to finding the solution.

The first question I want you to think about is your personal definition of inspiration. Go ahead and write a few thoughts on how you define the term "inspiration." To help you, I would like for you to think about a time when you heard or watched something that connected to your emotions. Did you show a physical response by crying or changing your facial expression? Did you feel an emotional response? Did you feel a connection with what you heard or saw? After hearing and seeing the content, did it spark a feeling or thought to do something different in your life?

Inspiration

Now that you've written down your personal views on inspiration, I want you to take two to three minutes to review it. Embrace what you wrote and see if you would change anything. If you're feeling confident you identified how you would define inspiration correctly, then we can continue.

The reason we started off with writing your personal view and definition of inspiration is because when you're in a leadership position, one of the biggest challenges is inspiring your team to go above and beyond. As I stated in the exercise above, the ability to connect with another individual and to spark an emotional or physical response is key when it comes to figuring out how you can inspire your team through your leadership.

Go above and beyond! The boss wonders why the reward, compensation, or acknowledgment doesn't happen when we see our teams or individuals go above and beyond. I want you to put yourself in this situation with your direct leader. Have you always been acknowledged or rewarded for going above and beyond? If you answer truthfully and if that answer is no, then have you realized that your team right now may be asking the same question? I pose these questions to you: Have you taken the time to stop, reflect, and embrace your teams by recognizing them or letting them know the work they are doing is inspiring and is helping to lay a foundation of great success that will sustain the organization for a brighter future? When was the last time you offered a single act of gratitude by stopping to thank your team or showing them they mean more to you than they realize?

What's a better way to show your team they matter than by acts of pure kindness and appreciation? The next exercise I would like you to embrace is to come up with five ways you can show your team, your peers, or whomever you may interact with a form of gratitude. Take as much time as you need because once you've finished writing these five bullets, we'll expand on actions that can bring these ideas to life.

Actions of Appreciation

If you didn't come up with all five, that's okay, but I want to challenge you to ensure you have at least three actions you feel confident about. If you don't have three, let's pause for a couple of minutes and go back to see what you can come up with. In fact, I want to share what my five were, and feel free to use them yourself.

1. Arrive early before all employees, stand at the entrance, and welcome every person into the workplace.

2. If it's appropriate to do, high-five at least ten employees or peers and tell them you're happy to see them.

3. Recognize birthdays or work anniversaries in a way that makes them fun. Buy a cake and personalize it.

4. Take time throughout the week to have personal one-on-one recognition with your teams. Pull them aside and show sincere appreciation for their contributions.

5. If you hold meetings or huddles with your teams, find a way to have interaction instead of doing all the talking yourself. Tell a joke or do a trivia question of the day.

When I began to implement these five actions into my routine, the engagement I noticed from everyone on the team started to increase. The results were seen through the sales and customer comments that started to pour in, as customers seemed much happier with all the levels of service and employees were willing to help other teammates much faster than before. I had more employees pull me aside and let me know they truly appreciated my actions of taking time to make work an enjoyable experience. They looked forward to coming to work every day.

I'll also share that I failed to win everyone in the organization over, for there were those who didn't want to change their ways or engage with positive progress. These were the individuals who didn't stay long with the company because they chose to display negativity instead of positivity. In fact, there was peer pressure from others who became tired of their unwillingness to be team players that led them to look for other jobs. In the long run, they were never going to make it with me, so by my creating a positive work environment, it led to weeding out the negativity.

Now, if you're reading the list I provided and you think it seems way too simple, cheesy, or even plain, then I want to share a bit of great information: gratitude doesn't have to be expensive, nor does it need to be given in an extravagant manner that comes across as arrogant. Giving away cars, trips, and copious amounts of money is fantastic, but if that's the goal, then I'd tell you to sign up for a game show on TV. The gratitude and appreciation we receive when we award nice gifts and expensive trips can be a rewarding experience, but not every company or organization can afford to give away such gifts. This is why small gestures of care and thanking our teams and individuals for the work they do are crucial and must be done daily and effectively in order to succeed.

Think about a time you felt you weren't recognized. Maybe you were asked to deliver on a tight timeline or even given an impossible project, but you came through and delivered an outstanding result. Your leader found ten other things to do besides showing gratitude or taking time to pull you aside and give you individualized thanks for your work. Reflect on those times, including if you're facing it now. I want you to really embrace the focus over that feeling. This situation left you uninspired or defeated. Remember how we talked about our minds in lesson one and how powerful it is to control our actions, feelings, and emotions? When you think about these challenging times, I want you to focus on that feeling. It doesn't feel great, and it may even anger you a little, but don't get too angry. Just reflect for a few moments. Embrace the emotions because when you understand what your teams feel, this will change your mind to understand the rationale clearly and to embrace the proper actions you need to take in order to effectively lead your team.

The key takeaway here is that for every feeling you experience in your daily life, I promise you that your team is experiencing the exact same emotions or situations. Too often do we forget that our teams are human. They aren't numbers, and they aren't sales or figures on a spreadsheet. The leader we report to is human as well. They feel just like we do, they get frustrated just like we do, and they enjoy recognition just like we do. So what's the difference, then? The difference is how you respond as the leader by inspiring your team to go above and beyond the normal call. You can inspire your teams through simple interactions and demonstrations of earnest gratitude. Be the servant leader you need to be, and display what it means to care for another human being.

The goal here is to understand that inspiration doesn't need to always be a heart-wrenching story about your past or something you overcame that made you the leader you are today. We will cover those topics in a later chapter, but for now, understand that inspiration comes from your words and actions every single day. It's the ability to connect with those you work with. Are you able to draw out those emotional reactions that will better them and the work they provide? One great arena for this practice is that of meetings; a meeting can truly be the breeding ground for creative ideas or sparking thoughts of great, valuable solutions to business problems.

Creating energy in meetings, interacting on a daily basis to kick off the day, or breaking through the normal routine can almost reenergize a team that may not be focused. Think about the last time you walked away from a meeting that left you amped and ready to tackle the day. Did you laugh or hear a motivational story you could relate to? Laughter from jokes and trivia questions will show a team a change in the culture for the better by displaying a sincere demonstration of trying to make work a more energetic environment. A bonus is if there are new members on the team. This is a win-win because what could be a better message to send about the culture to the new employees? Turnover in a company begins on day one, and if the leader doesn't ensure that every new employee is engaged and keeps the excitement of starting a new position, then a hefty cost will come down the road when the person decides to leave for a position that adds more value to their personal life.

One area that can create a sense of unity, giving back, and energy in your culture is if you're fortunate enough to work at a company that has a focus on charity or serving the community. If so, then there are projects that you, as the leader, can spearhead to inspire your teams. This idea isn't new and, in fact, is quite common, but I want to pause for a moment and ask you to think about this question. At any time this quarter or fiscal year, have you, along with your team, served a purpose for the community? What about giving proceeds to a charity?

An easy example of this was a cleanup day I did with my team. We took a stretch of road that wrapped around our parking lot and removed trash, cut down branches, and fixed areas that looked really rough. What this did was give the customers who drove in a great feeling about the business they supported because they saw the team cleaning up the area. It showed that my team took a high level of pride in where they worked. Another accomplishment was this created a great opportunity for team members to work with people they may not interact with daily.

I understand you may not be in a position of power to make these types of calls, but that shouldn't stop you from inspiring others by being the first one to step up and act. Create office challenges that are easy for most to take part in. The biggest one I used in the past was "penny wars." This is where you set up a mason jar, plastic jugs, or boxes with a small slit on the top to collect pennies. The goal is to drive engagement by seeing which team can collect the most pennies or which business or company matches the total number of pennies collected. I have seen this work in small and large businesses, and the cool part is you don't have to use pennies; you can choose any denomination of money. The goal here is to get the team inspired by serving kindness. The charities we donated to were local ones that supported the community, and some were military veteran organizations.

One particularly important takeaway here is that when you lead the project or a project is put together by the team you manage, *do not* be the "one task wonder" leader! If you're asking yourself what that means, then I'm more than happy to give you an example. Have you ever seen the pictures in magazines or company-shared photos of the smiling individual in a business suit, holding a hammer, shovel, paintbrush, or whatever tool they have as they pose for a photo opportunity? Did you wonder if those leaders stayed around to help with the project or if they were there strictly for the PR of the company?

There is a time and place for those types of opportunities, but the respect level increases tenfold when you get down and dirty with the team no matter how high your rank is on the ladder. In fact, the higher your rank is, and the more involved you are, the greater the team's sense of purpose will be when they see you're willing to truly stand by the mission and purpose of the call to action.

The last focus exercise is for you to challenge yourself to create three ways you're going to inspire your team with a mission focus project. Are you going to clean up a local park or a nearby school? Can you provide meals to those who are at a shelter, or can you help with a community project in your city? Can you help with a race that is sponsored for a charitable cause? If these ideas are ones you would like to use, please write them in the space below.

Project Ideas

I challenge you to start with one of these three ideas and act on it. Take the first steps to be the leader by communicating the mission you're looking to achieve. This may take some time and often will have setbacks or roadblocks, but the growth of planning an event from beginning to end will create a sense of ownership and inspiration that your team and leaders will recognize.

The final takeaway I want to create for you is the road map for how to act and own a project by serving. Nothing feels more satisfying than sitting down to take a deep breath and look back to see the success from a place of purity. When you genuinely care about a mission that will inspire your team and show them you're willing to serve a higher cause than the typical role of the "boss," your mind and actions will condition you to do more acts of this nature. Never forget that your business, no matter the field, has a common theme: people. People are needed in order to run a company, an organization, a charity, a firm, a practice, or whatever you want to call it. It takes people, and those people who are involved with it need to be inspired and feel they serve a higher value than what they are called to do.

As in lesson one, finish this chapter by saying the following phrase three times: *serve below and win above!*

LESSON THREE
ROUTINE MAKES ALL
THE DIFFERENCE

Let's do a quick recap of lesson one and two. We learned that leadership starts with you and that sharpening your mind is key to figuring out how you'll lead. You must take time to see the areas where you need to grow and further embrace the ones that are already strengths for you.

When your mind is sharp and focused on your team like we discussed in lesson two, the time is coming when you can truly serve and fulfill the mission of becoming a servant leader. We focused on creating a new energy in the organization and in your personal time with your team. What steps are you going to take to ensure that your team is inspired, and you're focused on serving them? Remember, that takeaway challenge was to focus on getting involved in the community or a local project with your team. Again, if you need to take a few minutes to go back and review your lesson one and two questions, please take the time to do so before moving on to this new section.

Having the knowledge and resources to create an empowering work environment and organization is a building block in the great foundation of becoming a servant leader. But what happens when there is no routine and you and your organization feel lost? Routine can and will dictate how well an organization functions. It can create great growth and revenue along with engaged teams, but there is a great cost when there is no routine.

In this section, we're going to break down the importance of routine not just from a work perspective but from a personal one as well. I want you to walk away feeling extremely comfortable that you understand the importance of routine and can create one. You want to be able to create a routine for your teams or organizations, but you also need to have the knowledge to teach and train them to become self-dependent with their own routines.

There is a principle when creating routines that must be remembered: focus on solutions. The main objective you should aim to achieve when you create patterns of habit in your life is to provide solutions. These solutions can begin to ease the "time robbers" that take you away from being successful. There needs to be a purposeful mission for creating routines. When I had the best success, my routine was mission driven, was specific, and created the solutions I needed to keep gaining success.

I would like for you to take five minutes and write down what a routine means to you. Don't worry about being accurate because this is a self-journey and the important takeaway is your self-identification of your personal leadership. To help prepare your mind for the task at hand, think about when you were a kid growing up. I'm sure there was a certain schedule you followed where you had dinner, cleaned up your toys, brushed your teeth, washed your face, and then crawled into bed for the night. This is a perfect, simple example of routine. However, what does routine mean for you in terms of your daily life?

What Does Routine Mean to You?

If you need more time to write down your thoughts, then please make sure you finish and capture everything before moving on. Now I have a couple of follow-up questions. Did you think that was a hard question? Was it easy to think about what a routine is and to put that thought into words? Do you feel that someone who never knew what a routine was could read and understand the flow of how your thoughts progressed? Take a couple of moments and think about those questions in order to get your mind warmed up and the gears turning.

When I think about what a routine is, it becomes clear that routine to me is the train that takes the track of success. To me, no matter if a train is hauling passengers or products across the country, it has a mission. A train is a resource used to achieve success in a mission, meaning it must follow a routine on the guided course in order to reach its destination. It needs to follow a clear path, but along the way, there may be a change in direction, forcing the train to redirect back to a path. That routine of understanding the redirection will keep the train on course to meet its destination with success.

However, before the train can leave the station, there is a routine a conductor will take in order to ensure the equipment being used is safe, is reliable, and won't create any surprises along the way. The train inspector has an extremely important role to play in the safekeeping of whatever the train is required to do. Think of yourself as the conductor and your personal life as the train. In order to live a meaningful life, we create routines to have the feeling of fulfilling our purpose. In your career, the same principle is applied.

I found that my team was the most successful when the routines that were set up were clear and the foundation of consistency that was put in place day after day was able to be executed at a high level. At first, setting the foundation was extremely hard, and I came close many times to not sticking to what I was focused on. Creating a routine will be a daunting task; I promise you will feel like the train is stuck at the station. The reason it was hard for me to create structure for my team was due to the fact that I wasn't following a routine. I had great ideas and many thoughts about getting work done faster, but what I failed to do was create a stable pattern that anyone on the team could follow. If I had taken the time to establish a well-thought-out routine, I probably wouldn't have wanted to give up so easily.

Because of this, my team saw there wasn't a lot of movement, and they may have even been wondering if I knew what I was doing. This doubt spilled into my thoughts and started to stall my efforts because I was very scattered. I had a perfect train but was failing as the conductor.

Before we move too far down the track of routine, let's take a few steps back and begin with your personal routine. The reason we need to begin with your personal routine is because what you practice in private will carry into public. When you see someone who is successful and they seem to have all their stuff together, know that often behind that success is the power of a great personal routine. When you focus and develop your mind into a powerful resource like we learned in lesson one, it can help you create the focus needed to develop a routine for yourself. But what exactly does that look like? Are you able to recognize that routine right now and what your own routine looks like?

Let's start with our first focus: understanding our personal routine. Take five to ten minutes to write your personal routine below. Please be as detailed as possible in terms of the order in which you do these events. For example, you wake up at 6 a.m., read for thirty minutes, have breakfast for twenty minutes, take a shower, then get dressed for the day. Include all the time it takes to complete the tasks.

Please focus only on your normal routine from the time you wake up until you stop for lunch. If you need more time to write everything down, please take that time, as the more you put into these focus activities, the more you will take away.

Time	Activity

Now, after you have written out your routine, I want you to take three to five minutes to read over it. The reason I want you to review is because often our minds will skip important events the first time we write down our thoughts, as we're rushing to remember as much as we can.

How hard or how easy was that exercise for you? If you're familiar with forming routines, then most times that exercise is quite easy. However, if you don't have a routine to stick to each day, then the exercise can be more difficult because we tend to write down random activities we do instead of a focused routine., reflect to lesson one. To understand how our minds, work, we need to visualize what we process in terms of thinking. The same principle goes for writing down your routine. I need you to visualize what you believe is your routine and ensure you accept the thoughts you wrote.

I want to share an example of what my routine looks like. It may be helpful to see what I did, compare it to what you're doing, and take away helpful aspects for yourself. This was my routine from the time I woke up to the time I left home to head to the office.

Time	Activity
5 a.m.	Woke up and took a couple minutes to stretch and warm up for the day.
5:15 a.m.	Had breakfast and looked ahead to what I would have for lunch. Packed my lunch or planned on buying.
5:30 a.m.	Made sure I was getting ready for the day no later than this time.
6 a.m.	Made this a starting point to read a devotional or listen to something positive.

| 6:05 a.m. | Did a final walk-through to ensure I had everything I needed. |
| 6:45 a.m. | Arrived at the office with plenty of time to spare to meet with my leaders. |

Now, the routine above will likely be quite different from your personal morning routine. I recognize that many have children they must ensure are fed, dressed, and ready for the school bus or babysitter. Some of us live in larger cities where taking the daily commute resource is our way to work and other places we travel. The point is that you should plan for and anticipate every action because it'll keep you focused on your goals and accountable.

Nevertheless, no matter what you must do in order to arrive at your destination in the morning, there is a routine to help guide you and your actions to guarantee you reach it safely and on time. However, if you find that most times you're running your routine down to the last minute and are often late or cutting it close, then a change is needed. There is a glitch in the process that is causing you to fumble or not reach the finish line in the time you need.

Take a moment to really focus on the principle we're discussing. When you feel rushed and not as organized as you wish you were, this can be dangerous for your future growth if you don't make the changes needed in order to better yourself with a routine that ensures you're achieving the success you desire.

As you become stronger in your mind and your personal routine is putting you in the best position to succeed, then your professional routine will also see the success. Both will play a significant role in your life as you spend time at work and at home. These two locations take up ample amounts of time that we account for in our day-to-day lives. I would like for this understanding to be a learning moment for you to look at where you can improve with your personal routines.

What can you change or where can you include more time in order for you to operate at a higher level or feel more accomplished about your life? Often, the most successful leaders incorporate a way to read, learn, and study something to add value for their personal wealth or the skills to expand their foundation. I challenge you to step back and think about what and where you can add something that will help your personal growth to achieve success.

Now that we have focused a productive amount of energy and mental practice on your personal routine, we can switch to your work routines and focus on the impact a great routine can have on a successful leader. Great leaders know where they need to be at what time and how long they can expect to be there.

Have you ever wondered why those who speak at corporations and conferences are booked at an expensive rate? It's because they have built a foundational wealth in their routine that has gained them experience and skills they can use to go forth and present. This makes leaders and those who influence highly sought after as subject experts.

Early in my career, I was eager and aimed at creating strong routines, or so I thought. It turned out that I was only focused on the appearance that I had a great work routine, but in truth I was fumbling to look like I did. I struggled with work routines because like most new leaders, I was inexperienced and still had the training wheels on while I figured things out. In my first assignment as a site director, there were roughly twenty to thirty tasks that had to be completed daily and weekly in order to stay in compliance. Of course, as the rookie, I was getting called out for not having everything done on time. The big reason why is because I told everyone to just do it, but I failed to set a foundation for them to follow.

The problem here can be a lofty miss, as even without knowing what you don't know, there still needs to be a routine. There is a practice of patience to observe and figure out that each day you need to show a progression of creating a stable routine for you to embrace. In my first thirty days of joining a new program, company, or location, what I didn't realize was that after day one, I could have very easily begun to design a routine based on what I did know that would have helped me set a foundation to build upon.

Here is where the work routine training will help line up some key practices you can implement to set up your success. Take the mistakes I made and channel them for you to be successful. Starting at a new place of employment can be exciting, but we want that excitement to carry into becoming a professional or the go-to person.

Let's end this lesson by saying the following aloud three times: *precise, practice, and perfection.*

LESSON FOUR
THE BEGINNER'S ROUTINE

I t's your first day of your new career or recent promotion! Many of us have been blessed enough to experience this amazing feeling of accomplishment, gratitude, and hopefully the humility to realize the opportunity you've been given. I'm going to take a couple swings at how you felt the night before. More than likely, you were daydreaming about how the day was going to start. You probably ironed and laid out your clothes. I imagine you walked around your kitchen and ensured you had breakfast lined up so there was enough time to make it for your early arrival on the big day.

How did you sleep the night before? Can you recall all those emotions and thoughts swimming through your head? Can I be successful in this role? Am I ready? If you're like me, you more than likely talked yourself out of the job and back into it a hundred times. It's okay if you did. It means we care to a degree that we don't want to let ourselves down, let others down, or be a disappointment to the company or individual that took the chance on us. However, I imagine your routine the night before was something of perfection and beauty. Do you treat every night and day the same as that time? Do you wake up and feel the same excitement that you're ready to set out and conquer the business?

If you answered no, then that's okay, and, in fact, most of us would need to say no. Imagine, though, if you did treat every night and day the same as that exciting first one. When I headed into my first director role, I was nervous, and I was pretty sure I left footprints embedded in the floor from pacing back and forth. I wanted to make sure I had everything lined up. I put my shoes by the door for quick access. My keys were staged on the table leading into the house so I could grab them and not waste any time.

The point I want you to focus on is that a routine, no matter why you chose to do it, can and does make all the difference on how quickly you achieve success and career goals. The best leaders understand the importance of having a successful routine that guides their time and keeps them from straying toward activities that would make their efforts unsuccessful in any measure. They are protective of their time.

Going back to the end of chapter three, we're going to focus on the importance of establishing a strong routine for your new career. This practice can really help you build a strong foundation to set your footprints in the channels of success.

Before we get started, I want you to take five minutes and write down your current work routine. Build this routine based on a rough estimate of when you arrive and the time you leave on an average day. You don't have to be extremely detailed, but be fair and give yourself enough to work with. Think about this exercise and how you wrote out your personal routine. Think about the little things, and ensure that some time is accounted for those actions, such as the time you spend on your breaks, the time you take to talk to peers, and so on. Don't worry if you don't use all the lines.

Time	Activity

The action items above will be the starting point, and as in lesson one, the goal is to visually see how we think and how our mind operates and processes ideas. This is extremely important when it comes to routines because most people will walk through their morning routine in their head, but I guarantee there is a missed step or action they forgot. The goal here is to supply a well-oiled machine in terms of a successful routine and for it to become second nature to us.

When you start a new career, a promotional position, or even a new position that may be a lateral move, the one key principle to remember is your old routine will only carry over limited aspects into your new role. I think back to those days in my career, and I see where the gaps were and the misses I didn't correct. I didn't have the benefit of knowing what I know now.

When I took my first leadership role, I eventually learned to create basic routines that helped me ground myself. However, as I progressed into later assignments, the challenges required new styles of completing the work. This is why only certain parts of your routines will carry from position to position. My first assignment was a smaller role in terms of how many people I was leading, so a lot of my interactions were much more personable. As the assignments became larger, I had to make adjustments in order to effectively lead tasks. That's the beauty of this book—I can share my shortcomings in the hope it will steer you down a more successful path.

Day one can be very nerve racking even before you pull into the parking lot. If you can drive the day or night before to your new work location (if it is new), it'll allow you to gather a feel for how long it'll take and what obstacles may get in your way. Keep note of the following questions: How many railroads do you cross? How many stoplights are there? If there's traffic, how long will it take to clear the intersection? Is there another route if you're running late? Is this the fastest route? I strongly recommend starting your routine from here. Don't wait until the first day of the new job to try it. Give yourself the confidence that you will succeed in your efforts by ensuring you make it to your destination accordingly.

Knowing the details of everything that could derail you from setting an example by always being punctual can dictate the level of credibility you have. You're setting personal and professional examples by when you arrive at work. I always admired those leaders I worked for whom I never could beat to work. They knew I was on the prowl to move up and do more, but they always humbled me by beating me to work no matter how hard I tried.

In fact, the only way I could have beat them was to start showing up the night before, but that would have been a complete waste of time and resources just to prove a point. The secret I didn't know was they knew every detail it took to ensure they could leave their houses and be to work before me. The key was they weren't focused on beating me and didn't care if they did. This was an established practice for them, and no one would derail that routine.

The reason I never beat them is because I was so focused on it that I wasn't paying attention to the solution—my routine. I wasn't stopping to learn the valuable practice of how a well-guided routine can set you up for success. I didn't take the time to evolve and become comfortable with setting a solid practice and being consistent with it.

You need to find what works for you and what fits into your lifestyle. There is no one size fits all when it comes to establishing a well-rounded work routine. The goal for you is to know that your time is valuable, especially when you're leading teams. If you derail yourself and don't quickly take note, this can be the deciding factor of a project finishing on time or late. There were situations in my career where I found myself guilty of this happening. In fact, the biggest one was a special assignment I was selected to do in order to launch a new product. I was excited and eager to prove myself, and when the assignment came down the pipe, I threw all my time at it. What is important to understand is that the processes my team used at the time were going to impact how well this product launched.

My failure was that I got off track from my normal routine and how I led the team to execute it came at the cost of the launch being delayed. I now know that if I would have stayed focused and stuck with the consistency of what I was doing, I wouldn't have missed the deadline. The team didn't fail; I failed them. Learn from what I did wrong. Understand that you must establish some ground rules in your beginning stages, which will carry you down a successful path.

Let's end this lesson with saying the following aloud three times: *perfecting time to perfect my routine, perfecting time to perfect my leadership.*

LESSON FIVE
THE INFORMATION GAME

I t's safe to say we can now move past your routine to help you succeed as a new leader and begin to turn our focus toward knowing and not knowing what you know. The reason I suggest this theme for lesson five is because in the beginning of your journey as a leader, this behavior can be used to grow your credibility and inner strength in your leadership confidence. For me, this was a precious time when I started to understand that the information, I needed to know would produce itself from how my routine manifested when I arrived at work.

I aimed to arrive early in order to find the knowledge I was lacking, and I always loved this practice. The reason was there were shift handoffs I knew I needed to see to understand the full circle of life within the business. If there were issues I could face in the future, I wanted to ensure I knew what was going on from handoff to handoff with all leaders. I needed to know for certain that when I was getting information relayed to me or had to speak about the process of information, I would not be misguided.

As a new leader, this is a big miss that many individuals think they can fake their way through to make it seem like they have a clue as to what is really taking place. I'm sure you've seen that one peer or employee who always seems to have the answers but is absent from the majority of the business. When they speak, you think to yourself, "How would you know?" You can set yourself apart by being authentic when you understand the importance of knowing and being able to speak about these types of situations when a question arises. What you need to grasp in order to succeed is discovering what practice best suits you.

Taking selective notes or finding key facts that will trigger you to look further for the information at a later date is an integral tool for growth in your leadership. There is a humbling aspect of being a new leader where you need to feel comfortable about not knowing all the details of the job. Find a way to feel comfortable with producing quick notes to follow up on later. Something I always tell myself is that every expert was once a student and every pro was once a rookie. I know it can feel frustrating to not produce the results you're aiming for, but that feeling of discomfort can be an opportunity for character growth.

One method I always loved and learned from a leader I worked for early in my career was his practice of throwing away sticky notes before going home. He made it a focus as he traveled throughout the day that if he came across a question he didn't know the answer to or needed to find more information about the business, he wrote it on a sticky note and kept it in his notebook. At the end of the day, he took a couple of minutes to review those sticky notes, and before he went home on Friday, he made sure all those sticky notes had an answer or he found the information he needed.

I used that same guided practice for my day-to-day operations and tours. I made sure that before I left for the day, I had thrown away all my sticky notes or planned to follow up the next day to complete what was carried over. I know most of us use cell phones, but I want to encourage you to write down your questions, as it forces stronger memory recognition to retain the information.

The "information game" is a game changer when it comes to proving your leadership. How often have we worked with bosses who gave generic answers when we asked a question or needed guidance? It was always a pleasure to hear those nice, prerecorded phrases coming from a robot, right? I don't think so, and nothing will kill your credibility with your teams more than if you can't provide some helpful information or wisdom. There is a divide between supplying incorrect information and being humble enough to own up to not knowing the appropriate response at the time. Again, ensure you take the time to research and provide valuable solutions to your teams.

I want to branch off from the sourcing of information and guide us toward another resource for creating a good information routine to acquire the knowledge you need. Ask yourself, where do *I* look for the information? This can be a difficult task for some individuals because I've seen too often that people will stick with the first piece of information they hear and believe it. They don't take the time to challenge the information and look a couple of levels deeper to see if it's valid.

Do you remember the telephone game where you start out with a phrase and then deliver it across twenty people one by one, with the last person ending up with a completely different message? When you're in a position where you give or receive information, look to the source, and take a second to digest and decipher after hearing it. I can tell you that many mistakes early in my career were based on the first piece of information I heard.

Here's an example of a problem employee in the organization who I thought was causing trouble. The problem was I was only listening to their direct leader and failed to look further into the source of the information I was given. I didn't stop and dig deeper, which ended up causing this individual to leave. Turns out, I lost a great contributor. If only I had taken the time to dig deeper. It took me a few years to really learn to listen with intent and pick apart the facts from the lies. My advice is to learn to find the facts and recognize the difference between what's valuable and what isn't.

How do you decipher the facts from the rest of information? Before we move forward with the practical piece you can implement, I want you to write down how you decide if someone is giving you factual or nonfactual information. Take five minutes and jot down some thoughts. Really think about those specific conversations you can pull from where you later found out the information you received was incorrect. What clues would you look for now?

Key Indicators

Perhaps one of the toughest aspects of leadership is making decisions or gaining knowledge based on conversations. I often think of salespeople who have perfected the game of persuasion and crafting how the context of the words is laid out to resonate with you or capture your attention. There's nothing wrong with this if it's done in the right context and at the appropriate time. Sometimes the people we interact with are phenomenal salespeople but aren't in the sales game. So what does that mean?

Think about the relationship between you and that person you already know and feel comfortable with. You're already apt to listen to them with a stronger confidence and with the intent to retain information more than with someone you've just met. What if that person you "trust" misled you?

A great technique to use when you need to find information or decipher information that is brought to you is playing the "skeptic" game. I often used this approach to make sure I didn't buy right into the first thing I heard every time. When I heard information, I asked simple questions to dig deeper. If someone said, "Did you hear about Joe Schmo and what he did last week with the sales report?" I would reply, "No, I didn't. What happened?"

The key here is not to get into a gossip train, but by acting as if something didn't happen, I opened more information for myself to retain in order to figure out what stance I needed to take. When you offer a rebuttal or say the opposite, the person is much more inclined to prove why their information is accurate. Leave room for open-ended questions.

After the person finished and I felt I had heard enough to make a rational decision, I would often say, "Wow, thanks for your point of view. Definitely something new." This suggested the conversation was done and there was no need to carry on further.

Another approach that can be used is the "why" approach, which is a great method to dig deeper into the context of the conversation. When the information is provided, reply with "Why?" or "Why would they say/do that?" This provokes the person to go deeper into the conversation. This approach has been a long-time practice of many great companies and leaders over the years.

I will say, however, it's often forgotten and there are few who still use this practice. If you haven't done this drill before, then I want to challenge you to do this in a conversation. It doesn't need to be about specific work situations. It can be a casual conversation but use the why approach to see how much information you can discover. Once you have done this, I want you to come back to write down how you felt about asking why. Were there any times you were tripped up by asking?

How Did You Feel?

The final piece I want to cover in finding and obtaining information is when to take it to your direct leader and how to present it. In my career, I had many direct reports that I felt so eager to run with and provide information for myself because our goal as leaders is to contribute. We want to feel like we can provide solid solutions and insightful information that will render us valuable to our company. This, however, can go horribly wrong when the proper time isn't taken to learn the appropriate timing of providing the information to your direct leader.

I'll admit I was guilty of jumping the gun and rushing to provide "earth-shattering" information to my direct leader, which caused more headaches down the road. I found myself being the "hero" of the day or hour but later having to explain why the information I provided didn't come to 100 percent fruition. In most cases, this happened when my team was focused on selling to a large client. They would let me know this deal was potentially going down, and I'd get super eager and call my boss right away. Well, often the deal would either backfire or get postponed for a long period of time. Don't always rush to speak.

One way to protect yourself is to push the information in an open dialogue form. Approach your direct leader with a "Hey, do you have a minute? I heard this piece of information, and I want to get your thoughts." This approach helped shape my future conversations to be much more impactful. I was able to feel more confident in going to my leader and presenting information or asking great questions without jeopardizing my ability to look competent.

To end this lesson on information, I want you to know this is extremely tough and will definitely test your willpower. We always want to be the hero in the room or provide the quickest information possible to show we're amazing, but please take the time needed to ensure everything is correct and important. There is no safer practice of patience than training yourself to digest and decipher information in order for you to guide a decision with confidence.

Let's finish this lesson with saying the following aloud three times: *I will be truthful. I will be knowledgeable. I will be accurate.*

LESSON SIX
THE SHADOW OF YOUR LEADERSHIP

Imagine it's a bright, sunny day and you're walking on a sidewalk or road or driving down the highway. They both present the image of casting a shadow as the sun looks down upon the example environment. How does this relate to leadership, specifically your personal leadership? You also cast a shadow larger than you may realize. This principle is frequently overlooked when we become established in our roles as leaders. How often have you had a "generic" interaction with a high-level leader from your company or organization? Maybe even a professor or teacher? That interaction left you feeling confused or disappointed, as you were expecting a much richer conversation but realized there was no substance there.

We have all had those interactions where leaders have passed by without even saying hello or acknowledging our presence. Can you recall what it felt like? I imagine the feeling and thought was "There goes another corporate robot." Often, we see this scenario play out in movies, with leaders depicted as being stuck up or not mingling with the commoners. Sadly, there is truth with this picture in the real world. I recall trying to get myself known by networking with levels above me, and the quick and typical, "Hey, how are you doing?" was the only response I managed to receive.

I remember a time when our office received a visit from the regional team. I was so pumped to shine my talent and show off my knowledge in hopes they saw I was ready to be promoted. What I failed to understand was I only had ten seconds with no hope of sharing my talent. A name introduction was all I received. I hyped myself up only to be let down. Ten seconds caused me to second-guess if I was worth promoting.

The point is that you have the power to change how your shadow of position and leadership is cascaded. Imagine being the first person in your organization, facility, group, or class to stop and show a moment of compassion. It's often said that you should treat the janitor the same as the CEO, but how often is this advice used as a flashy statement but never implemented? Often, the great leaders we remember made some form of an impact or something they said stood out in our memory. There was a presence to them that we were able to relate to and understand the meaning behind their words. We should aim to emulate those leaders.

I want you to take five minutes and write out the characteristics of those you consider to have been excellent leaders. What made them great in your opinion? What stood out about the way they carried themselves? Was it the value they added to your conversations with them? Were they great when it came time to show empathy and understanding in situations?

Great Leader Characteristics

The reason I want you to write out what made them a great leader to you is to have you visually see and retain these actions. Most times with the actions we see others display and gravitate to, we forget that we can adapt to those modeled behaviors as well. Nothing is stopping us from self-improvement, but please make sure you can decipher the difference between copycatting and using the behavior in your personal way.

I want to take a moment and share my table of characteristics that I gravitated toward.

Great Leader Characteristics
They humbled themselves.
They communicated in simple terms.
They never belittled anyone.
I felt valued when I shared ideas.
I could relate to them on personal levels.
When I made mistakes, I felt comfortable speaking up.
They challenged me to not stop until I was done.

Often, we hear that the greatest form of flattery is imitation, but so is the shadow you cast of being "fake" when you completely change how you lead within one day.

Changing and implementing self-desired changes can take time to perfect and understand. Again, everything you do as a leader is covered by your shadow. If you make a radical change quickly, your team may not understand where it's coming from. Take time to understand that crafting your leadership is a long-term journey. There is no magical shortcut you can take that will make you change your human characteristics overnight. It takes time, simple as that.

A strong process that will help increase your presence as a well-established leader is getting to know your teams or organization. Take the time to know the problems that are troubling employees or the culture of the business. Now, this is much easier said than done. How hard is it to break the ice when you're not super familiar with everyone in your organization?

It's extremely hard because the longer you go without taking the respectable time to know your team or figure out the culture, the harder it will be for everyone to see the "light" of your credibility. An easy icebreaker tool is the practice of using note cards and writing information down about your team after a conversation. When you take the time to practice this process, you'll find that the ability to recall information about an individual will seem almost fluid and will help build a strong relationship with them.

While making my morning rounds in a facility, whenever I met someone new, I wrote down a quick fact or interesting point from that interaction. I obviously didn't do it in front of the individual, but I would step away and write down the information as soon as possible. At the end of the day, I went back through and reviewed the information on the notes to get to know my team.

The impact this made when I was working to establish relationships and connect with people made all the difference. I felt it was important to know at least something about everyone I worked with or the teams I was leading. I wasn't an expert on them, but I could at least start a conversation with them about a situation or experience that was taking place in their life.

I want you to embrace this same concept, and I'll issue a challenge for you to write down four team members or peers you haven't connected with and try the note card approach. I'll give you some space below to transfer those notes into this book as a reference.

Person	Interesting Fact

After you have completed the exercise, I want to know how these four interactions went for you. Did you feel uncomfortable at any point, or was it hard to really pay attention to what the person was saying? I think sometimes we focus so hard on the mission of gathering data that we often forget we're listening to learn about the person.

I hope that was a great networking or relationship-building drill, depending on whom you talked with. Again, the more you broadcast your shadow and take time to get to know people, the greater the foundation your leadership will be built upon. The great part is you can take this exercise and continue to apply it to every new team or promotion you take on.

Part of the shadow you cast is knowing when you need to address concerns, find solutions, or fix the culture of your business. A phrase I once heard that made all the sense in the world was that the culture of any business or organization is what the top leader allows. This is a powerful statement that has rung true with many companies and organizations over the years. Think about the world we live in. How many people do you know right now who are looking for a new career or a change or are just taking a break because they are burned out? A lot could and should be fixed by the top level if leaders were paying attention to what was happening.

I see many great organizations with the for-hire sign or advertisement posted, and one thought pops into my mind: what would happen if that company or leader took that money and invested back into finding out why they need to hire more staff? There could be a few good reasons, such as the business is growing, there is a franchise developing, or they are looking to move into a new sector and need to bring in additional experts in order to fill adequate roles.

I would venture to say that most need the hiring advertisements because they are blinded as to why their teams are leaving. This has everything to do with the shadow of the leader. Is that leader finding solutions and having meetings with all levels of the organization to find out where problems are happening and why morale may be down? Does the leader know where the strengths of the business are and where there may be an opportunity for training?

If this is a position you're in right now, then I want to encourage you to step back and look at what you could do better with your position. What keeps you from meeting with all your employees and spending time to get to the bottom of finding information that may lead you to the bleeding problem of why you continue to hire. It could very well be that leaders are afraid to hear the truth or feel that if they are given a problem, then they must provide a quick and swift solution.

Sometimes the best solution is just hearing and letting your teams vent about their frustrations. People often leave because they feel their voice isn't heard or appreciated. You must be able to use your ability to connect with people and show your team or company you're ready to listen to them. You are there to sit down and make yourself available to hear and provide feedback toward steps you can take as the leader to create a better experience for those individuals.

I want to offer a suggestion. Take the money from the advertising budget you set aside for hiring, and invest a portion of it back into your teams. Invest that money into showing them your appreciation for the hours they are putting in and their contribution to the company.

I'd even challenge you to see if that budget could equate to a pay raise for your team. Sometimes that little bit of focusing your attention on their problems and providing a wage increase can make all the difference. In fact, if you're truly in tune with your business or organization, then I'm sure there are multiple budgets you could cut to increase your team's wages. I understand you may not have that power, but I promise there is something you can do to get your team to commit back to the company. It all depends on how much you truly care to find the root cause of the problem and deliver a solution.

In closing out this lesson, I want to propose one last key takeaway exercise for you to have as a resource to reflect on. We talked about a couple different ways your leadership shadow casts onto the organization and the people in it. What are four takeaways you can implement right now in your life that will improve the culture? I want you to put a deadline to implement the actions on each decision you write down. Hold yourself to the deadline and be honest with yourself. This will create a sense of urgency for you to hold yourself accountable.

Action	Deadline

These action items represent so much more than just completing the exercise. They are a symbol of your leadership that you're willing to recognize so you can better your shadow and cast a brighter and more engaged culture for your organization.

Let's finish our lesson by saying the following phrase three times: *I see and know; therefore, I will and can change my shadow!*

LESSON SEVEN
LEAVE IT ALL OUT THERE

The final lesson I'd like to provide in this guide is what it means to leave it all out there. This last lesson comes more from the heart and not so much from textbooks, studying, or anything similar. Often, we forget what it means to be a leader, as the beginning journey is always so exciting and adventurous. As we grow into our role and develop from the rookie into the expert, we sometimes lose the basic principles of what made us successful in the first place. Remember, for every level is another devil, and those devils add up quickly in terms of the importance of your position.

Whether you are a third-line leader, second-in-command, or the top leader, the expectation of the work will feel hefty. The higher you move up the ladder, the stronger the expectations grow. I know I'm not telling you anything new, but we often need a reminder sent to us in a way we can visually see and process versus just hearing it. When we read, our minds process information differently than they do when we hear something. For some, just hearing the advice will make it click, and they will make that mental reminder of "Oh yeah. I need to make a change." Others will hear it and move on rather quickly because the business of the day amps up.

That's where I find beauty in guides like this book that can help slow down the leader to take the time to gain the important information needed. The hard part is committing time to read this book and to do the activities and thoughts. It's too easy to pass through this short read and discard the information, thinking it was of no use for you.

If you commit the time and effort to put what you read into practice, it will make a difference. That's why I wanted the last lesson to be leaving it all out there. We often hear that phrase in the sports world, competition, funerals, or celebrations. In leadership, however, leaving it all out there is a daily grind and takes the strongest mindset to wake up and reset to focus on ensuring you're motivating, making the right decisions, and creating those close relationships needed for growth.

The worst days you feel as a leader will be the best days of another leader's life. This is a key point I want you to highlight, write down, or do whatever you need to save that sentence. Humans are hardwired to look for protection, just like children find out a stove is hot after they touch it once and refrain from ever touching it again. As we grow, we develop this in our lives. Our minds are designed to protect us, and we often look out for ourselves.

In leadership this same principle is often seen, but those who can rewire their minds to think differently in terms of serving others come to great success. The best leaders I worked for always knew that the fastest way to their promotion was promoting others. Again, this is an easy concept to think about, but putting the actual theory into practice will require you to leave it all out there.

Let's finish this book with saying the following three times: *I will leave it all out there!*

IN CLOSING

At the beginning of the book, I asked how you would safely guide a room full of drowning victims under your command. We talked about the different ways you could go about getting the information to everyone. You could take the direct approach and be very forceful, as the situation is dire, or you could take the individualized approach and ensure everyone could understand your direction to the best of their ability.

That exercise was to get your mind comfortable with breaking down your processes and feelings in order to understand how your mind works and if you could persuade yourself to think differently if needed. Being able to recognize your patterns is key to evolving your growth.

While you grow in your confidence as a leader, the ability to understand how to serve below to lead your teams is crucial. People will always work for people, and the same token applies that people will leave people, especially in a work environment where they feel they aren't valued. Take the time to showcase how much you appreciate your team and how the work they do every day makes a difference in the mission you're trying to achieve. Think about your team's engagement as an investment.

If you personally lost $48,000, I imagine you would be all about searching for where the money went. Your team has the same value. They have much more to offer than the salary you pay them, but from a business standpoint, it's extremely costly to lose great talent when you don't value them. People work for people.

I can speak from experience when I was in the second levels of command and had leaders who loved how hard I worked but failed to invest in my talent and hunger for doing more. They were able to see that my hard work was growing their success, but they used it as leverage to keep me in fear of doing more. What I didn't realize was they needed me more than I needed them. People work for people when you treat them right. Remember, they don't need you as much as you think.

Motivating and inspiring people are key parts of being a successful leader, but make sure you can effectively lead them where you need to go. In lesson three, we reviewed the importance of having an effective routine to help guide you and keep you on the path of success. What does your personal routine look like in your life? Do you feel it can be cleaned up a little to hit the level of accomplishment you're aiming for?

Take the time to sit down and write out your schedule to see where you can add greater success and take away time robbers. This will strengthen your confidence and navigate you toward success more quickly.

After perfecting your personal routine to ensure you are where you feel comfortable, you need to establish your credibility in your new leadership role. The importance of lesson four about focusing on how you enter your workplace will build confidence from your teams in you that will be hard to break. Being a leader isn't just looking the part or taking the salary that comes with the promotion. It's truly ensuring you take the time to understand what you need to invest in knowledge and resources to fully serve your teams. How you enter your first leadership assignment will make your career a long-term success or failure. It all starts with day one.

Lesson five gave focus to knowing your information and how you choose to share your knowledge. During that lesson, we talked about the importance of being transparent with your team and knowing how to show vulnerability when needed. It's a given that you'll never have all the answers, and that's okay. People don't expect you to be all knowing, but they do expect you to lead with true north guidance and ethics. Never lie or mislead your team even when the pressure is on from your boss. The true measure of the leader in you will be determined by those extremely difficult situations. Will you crumble or prosper? Be the leader I know you can be, and stand tall when the room falls short.

Rounding out the guide was lesson six—the shadow of your leadership and influence. If you take nothing else away from this guide, just take this note. You will always cast a shadow further than you know when you lead people. Your team and those around them will always be studying and watching you. It's the burden of leadership.

Knowing this can be a blessing to a degree, as the opportunity you now have to change and impact lives is at the forefront of your thinking. Only you will determine who you talk to and who you spend time with, and if you're only creating a circle of people who "look" like you, then you will struggle to win with the team when the time comes. Be comfortable stepping outside of your comfort zone, and know where you need to put your shadow of influence.

For the last lesson about leaving it all out there, I really want you to immerse yourself in the words. *Nothing* I can do or say will help you if you choose to not leave it all out there. Being a leader is a blessing, a curse, a burden, an amazing gift, and a nightmare all at the same time. What you say and what you do will impact someone's life. You will always be the subject of dinner conversation when that employee goes home, as they will share how their day went with a family member or friend.

I promise you will be talked about, so why not make sure it's a positive conversation? You and I both know you'll never be able to please everyone, and that isn't a goal of leadership. However, you can be vulnerable and transparent with your teams. They'll respect your leadership and feel more apt to trust you.

The greatest foundation a leader can establish is the ability to connect with everyone in the organization and build a circle of followers who choose to follow not out of fear but out of confidence. When you enter the room, you either have to demand respect, or you'll have the ability to command respect. If you find yourself demanding attention from your team, then there is work to be done on your part. You need to figure out why and embrace the changes that may be needed in order to effectively lead your business or organization further.

Being a leader is a blessing, but it will require you to sacrifice a large part of your life to become a servant and a leader. If you choose to follow this path, then I can assure you there is no greater calling in life, and all you'll need to do is leave it all out there.

FINAL WORDS

I want to leave you with some final words. Everyone has a beginning date on their tombstone and an end date. There is no escaping this. The beginning date is the blessing of your birth on this earth, and the end date is the final stamp of your existence on earth. The dash in the middle, though, is your life. It's your story, and people will tell your dash based on how you lived. Make sure your dash is told the way you want it to be told. Take the time to embrace every beautiful moment you're gifted with; embrace every sorrow you find yourself fighting through. All these experiences are blessings in disguise, but we need to have the emotional intelligence to know that we'll make it and can make it. So, I say it again for the last time—ensure your dash is told how you want it to be remembered.

Stay blessed.

Made in USA - Crawfordsville, IN
10724_9780578291390
01.02.2023 1947